GOD

AND

NUMBERS

BY: NIA GUICE

1 4 8 2 3 10 9 6 5 7

WestBow Press books may be ordered through booksellers or by contacting:

WestBow Press
A Division of Thomas Nelson & Zondervan
1663 Liberty Drive
Bloomington, IN 47403
www.westbowpress.com
844-714-3454

Interior Image Credit: Nia Guice

All Scripture quotations are taken from The Holy Bible, New International Version®, NIV® Copyright © 1973, 1978, 1984, 2011 by Biblica, Inc.® Used by permission. All rights reserved worldwide.

ISBN: 978-1-6642-4720-8 (sc)
ISBN: 978-1-6642-4721-5 (e)

Library of Congress Control Number: 2021921012

Print information available on the last page.

WestBow Press rev. date: 06/18/2022

WestBow
PRESS®
A DIVISION OF THOMAS NELSON
& ZONDERVAN

1

4

GOD

8

2

AND

3

10

9

NUMBERS

6

5 BY: NIA GUICE

7

This Book Belongs To

_____

This book is dedicated to:

My Mommy and Daddy
My Sisters and Cousins
My Grandmas and Grandpas
My Aunties and Uncles
My God Parents
My Church Family
My Friends

Special dedication to:

Dr. Claybon Lea, Jr. my Pastor
Dr. Cindy Trimm, my Mentor

Illustrator Notes

I am Nia Guice, and I hope you enjoy my book. I want to show how God and numbers relate. My Grandmother (mama) explained to me how numbers can help us remember important biblical meanings. For example, the number 1 can relate to the first book in the Bible (Genesis NIV). I also wanted to help my friends learn their numbers 1-10 while they are learning scriptures in the Bible.

God Bless.

Genesis is the number ✝1 book in the Bible.

2

God made two great lights

Day

Night

The Trinity

Father Son HolySpirit

Father

God

Son   Spirit

God made the Sun, moon, and stars on the

4th Day

Sun   Moon   Star

God
Created
the
animals

on the 6th day.

God rested on
the 7th day after
He created the
World.

Proverbs

:34

Blessed are those who listen to me, Watching daily at my doors, waiting at my doorway.

Psalm 9:1

1.
I will give thanks to your Lord with all my heart.

Numbers 1-3

Numbers 10: 1-3

Practice

1 📖

2 ☀️ 🌙

3 ▲ ▲ ▲

4 ⭐ ⭐ ⭐ ⭐

5 🥖 🥖 🥖 🥖 🥖

6 🐢 🐢 🐢 🐢 🐢 🐢

7 🛏️ 🛏️ 🛏️ 🛏️ 🛏️ 🛏️ 🛏️

8 🚪 🚪 🚪 🚪 🚪 🚪 🚪 🚪

9 🦋 🦋 🦋 🦋 🦋 🦋 🦋 🦋 🦋

10 🎺 🎺 🎺 🎺 🎺 🎺 🎺 🎺 🎺 🎺

God and his numbers have meaning.

Don't forget

God and His numbers are special.

1 2 3 4

5 6 7 8

9 10

Practice

1
2
3 4 5
6 7 8 9 10

Resource Page

The Children's of Color Story Book Bible (2019)

Printed in the United States
by Baker & Taylor Publisher Services